AMAZING BABY SLEEP SECRETS

EMMANUEL OKELLO

ISBN 979-888569079-9

This book is dedicated to my beloved wife, the one single person who has made my success possible and has broght honor and nobility to the whole process

Contents

Preface

Amazing Baby Sleep Secrets - Fast And Effective Ways

If you are a new parent who is always struggling with his/ her baby's sleeping pattern, look no more. We have compiled a few easy pointers about how to make a baby sleep on time. So, without wasting any time, let's get started.

Before starting, you must understand that every baby is different. Don't compare your baby's sleeping or eating habits with another. With time and proper techniques, your baby will also master the art of sleeping through the night without a daily battle.

Avoid rocking or bouncing your baby to sleep and use these proven methods on how you can get your baby or toddler to get the best nights sleep ever!

If you want a foolproof method of how to make a baby sleep, you need to start at an early age. One major mistake that parents make with their newborns is rocking, bouncing or soothing them to sleep.

Babies develop a dependency on these rocking and soothing motions and will not sleep without them. It becomes a big hurdle when babies get older. They will refuse to sleep unless they are rocked or bounced.

How do you overcome this? You put your baby down to sleep as soon as they

get drowsy. They will fall asleep on their own and this will help you in the
future. Babies who learn how to sleep by themselves continue to do so as
they get older and sleep throughout the night.

Early Bedtime

While trying to work out how to make the baby sleep at night without any
hassle, try putting your little one to bed early. Melatonin is a hormone that a
baby's body releases when he/she is around eight weeks old. It makes the
baby drowsy and ready for sleep according to the setting time of the sun.

If you ignore the timing and delay your baby's sleep time, the chances are that
your baby will get overstimulated and it will be harder for him/her to fall asleep.

So make sure you settle your little one down as soon as the sun goes down.

Naps Are Crucial

Day time naps are crucial for ensuring that your baby sleeps through the night
with ease. If you are coping with how to make baby sleep undisturbed, make
sure you set a day time napping schedule.

A baby that has had enough rest during the day automatically sleeps better at
night. When you skip your baby's naps in the hope of him/ her sleeping
throughout the night is a wrong approach. This increases their stress hormone
and as a result, the baby will keep getting up and won't be

able to fall asleep again. Don't believe us? Try it out for yourself.

Relax Your Mind

Parenting is anything but easy. It takes an obvious toll on your physical and mental health. So what if the baby isn't sleeping as much as you want him/her to? Give everything some time. Eventually, everything will fall into place, before you know it, your little one will be sleeping through the night without a hassle. Relax and stay positive. After all, you can only look after the baby if you are healthy yourself.

Parenting babies and toddlers can be very hard work. Especially if they are struggling to sleep.

How To Make Baby Sleep In Crib

Now that your child has grown up a bit and is ready to be shifted to the crib, you would need to have some information on how to make the baby sleep in the crib. Several factors need to be accounted for if you are to ensure your child's undisturbed sleep.

These factors are mainly small changes that you can make to ensure that your child gets a good night's sleep without any disturbances.

Dress Them Appropriately

The first thing you need to check on the list is that your child should wear clothes that comfort him while sleeping. A sleeper or pyjamas and a loose shirt would be great.

Temperature

Another factor to ponder upon is that you need to keep the temperature
moderate. If the temperature goes too low, your child won't be able to sleep as
they would feel cold.

If it rises too high, the kid would sweat and be uneasy and would not be able
to sleep properly. Hence it is vital to maintain a moderate temperature for your
little one.

Feed Them well

It is almost impossible for anyone, even the children, to sleep with a hungry
stomach. A person can't just stick to the thought of sleeping if they have not
eaten a sufficient meal lately.

Due to this reason, you should ensure that the mother has fed the child; or
the father if the child has started to take semi-solids or dairy milk. Once the
baby's stomach is full, he is more likely to get cosy and sleepy.

Set A Routine

If you want your child to sleep at a particular time and wake up at a specific
time as well, you will need to have a routine set. Every night, put them to sleep
at the same time and wake them up at the same time as each day.

This is crucial if you want to learn how to make a baby sleep in a crib.

According to researchers, it takes 21 days to develop a habit. Hence, if you are giving your child this pattern for 21 days straight, it is most likely that their bodies will adapt, and this would become their automatic routine.

Create A Suitable Ambiance

When sleeping or relaxing, a baby looks for an environment similar to that of the womb. You can make some minor changes to satisfy the baby. These are essential when learning how to make the baby sleep in the crib.

Firstly, you need to ensure that the lighting is low. The room should be semi-lit, and no rays of light should fall on the baby directly.

Secondly, you can use a soothing scent to make the environment sweeter and courteous to the child's needs.

Lastly, if you wish to know how to make a baby sleep in a crib, you need to pull off one final task. That is, to use a machine or play soft humming tunes on the phone to comfort the baby even further.

How To Get Your Baby To Sleep All Night

Many things have been proven to make babies feel relaxed, comfortable and to make babies sleep easily. Many women are worried about a single thing that is "how to get my baby to sleep all night"?

So here is a little guide for all the mothers out there who are facing problems regarding making their babies sleep at night.

Follow these
activities, make your babies sleep at the exact hour and in the right way so
that your baby can sleep more easily.
RELAXING BEDTIME ROUTINE:
Set a relaxing bedtime routine for your baby. Studies show that deciding a
bedtime routine for your baby before twelve months as your baby grows
taller, he or she will sleep in a better way.
If your baby falls asleep easier at night, he or she will sleep much longer at
night and will wake up a few hours later in the morning. This is one of the
best solutions to the problem, how to get my baby to sleep all night.
This thing will surely help you in making your baby feel relaxed and sleep
peacefully.
DISCOVER THE HIDDEN PATTERNS:
Many parents get excited when we talk about patterns when they start
recording or tracking baby's sleep patterns, but it does not have to be
complicated, there are many apps that you can download for free that can
easily track your baby's nap time.
The Reason for tracking your baby's sleep is that when you track your
baby's sleep for only a few days or a week, you will start seeing some
patterns out of this.
Here is an example of this procedure, so one mom that I

worked with
discovered that when her toddler went to bed before 9:00 p.m. He slept
later in the morning, and if the baby went to sleep after 9:00 p.m., even ten
minutes later, he would wake up a whole hour earlier.
She observed all this through tracking. Most of the women are worried
about how to get my baby to sleep all night. Discovering patterns will help
you out.
INTRODUCE NEW SLEEP ASSOCIATIONS:
Sleep associations are sleep props. There must be something that your
baby associates while falling asleep, and he wants that thing at bedtime,
which is not a bad thing. Sometimes sleep associations get a bad rap, but
this is to tell you that they are not bad.
You have independent and dependent sleep associations. Dependent
associations are that require you to help your baby to sleep, such as
feeding or some other things of entertainment.
Independent sleep associations are the sleep props that help your baby to
fall asleep but independent associations do not require your efforts so it
can be a pacifier if a baby can replace it by himself in the night, it might be
a lovely animal, etc.
This is the good thing that I can do to make my baby sleep all night with

new sleeping association tricks.
CONTINUOUS SNACKING HOURS:
Babies need to feed one or two times at night, which is nine months old, or
years even, you don't need to feed a baby more than that. Because after
three months, most babies don't have any kind of need to get fed after
every 1-2 hours.
After the completion of nine months, most babies can sleep for about ten to
eleven hours easily. Many moms are worried because of a single thing,
which is how to get my baby to sleep all night. You can choose a good
feeding time like one to four am.
So that your baby will get habitual of waking up in these hours only, and the
baby will adopt this routine without having any food all night
Complete Guide - Get your newborn into a routine
It is a universal fact that newborn babies sleep a lot. Mothers will
observe that their newborn will sleep for about 16-18 hours a day. It has
been found that newborn babies cannot live more than two hours.
Their sleep time will not last longer than this period. The newborn will
start developing good sleep habits from the fifth week. Newborns will
sleep less during the day and more at night.
Now at this point, he will develop natural circadian

rhythms (a process
that regulates sleep-wake cycle). How to get your newborn into a
routine? Many mothers ask the same question, here are a few things
that you can do:
Keep the Swaddle tight
All the newborns possess a startle reflex in which they feel they are
falling and wake during sleep. If you are wondering how to get your
newborn into a routine, try to make the newborn sleep in a tight swaddle.
Help your newborn to differentiate between day and night
Differentiate between day and night routine. During the day when she/he
wakes up, change her clothes, play with her, while feeding, talk to her,
switch on the lights, let her hear the noise in the house. At night take
newborns to the room, change him into a night suit, keep lights and
sound low, avoid talking while feeding him.
So this is one of many great ways for those women asking how to get
your newborn into a routine?
Keep the colour of the room low
Colours impact not only the layout of your room but also your body
hormones. If the room has sharp colours, it will be harder for your baby
to fall asleep.
Therefore while choosing the colour scheme to keep in

mind, blue is proven to be the best colour and yellow as the second-best colour to induce sleep; these colours have a soothing effect on the brain and hence impact sleeping and the sleep routine.

Dream Feed:

Dream feed means to feed your baby just before the mother goes to sleep. If you feed the baby just before you go to sleep, it will make the baby sleep longer and will help you also to have a sound sleep.

By feeding your baby at a certain time, you will increase the time of rest.

Your baby will sleep 3-4 hours. Make sure dream feeding does not increase the time more than three hours because newborn tummies are small, and they need to be fed after a few hours. Make a proper schedule and follow it.

Conclusion:

If you follow these simple steps consistently, you will never have to ask again how to get your newborn into a routine. If you don't support them properly and consistently, your baby might not ever sleep and wake on time.

Be patient and take care of the feeding time. Lastly, sing her or him a relaxing lullaby since several researchers have proven that

soothing
sounds induce peaceful sleep.
Parenting babies and toddlers can be very hard work. Especially if they
are struggling to sleep
Baby Sleep Routines
We have already discussed in detail how to make a baby go to sleep but
previously we were talking about infants. As the baby grows up, they
show changes in their habits and behaviour. This change occurs at
different stages and ages.
Once your child is around 3 months old, he will surely show signs of
changed behaviour. Once this happens, you would surely need to find
new methods of dealing with them. One of which is how to make a baby
go to sleep.
Change The Method
When we talk about changing the method, we do not refer to changing it
entirely, but rather making some modifications that would aid in putting
the child to sleep. To start off, we have to change the habit of putting the
baby to sleep.
If they are 3 months old and you have been treating them according to
the schedule, you should see that they put themselves to sleep. If this is
not happening, then you have not executed the routine

correctly.
Read our previous articles to get to know how to set the routine and how
to make the sleep routine for your child. But for now, let us focus on how
to make a baby go to sleep.
What you need to do is lookout for the signs of sleepiness that they
show. These would be yawning, rubbing their eyes, etc.
When you see this, put them into the crib/basket and play a soft tune.
You can pat their belly or stomach gently if you want. But otherwise, you
should not do anything else and let the baby put themselves to sleep.
Cuddle With Them
Instead of lifting them up and carrying them around, you should cuddle
with them. This would release beneficial hormones such as dopamine
which would reduce the stress level (if there is any) and make the baby
relaxed and calm.
Talk To Them
Research has proven that talking gently with the babies has a very
positive effect on their brains. They not only tend to be obedient but also
more cooperative and happy.
Saying phrases to them such as "Baby! It's time to wake up" and then
waking them up in a shower of gentle and light kisses is one of the best

ways to deal with the babies.
Hold Your Horses
As always, patience is a virtue in this scenario as well. You do not have
to rush to put them to sleep or get frustrated if they are unable to do so
by themselves. Allow them some time as you did before and they will
surely adapt to this new method as well.
If you remain calm, give the baby some space, and follow the steps
mentioned above, the process of how to make a baby go to sleep would
be much easier. Not just easier but it would also be much quicker than
you expect.
.
Baby Sleep - Things To Avoid
In search of finding the best answer about how to make my baby
sleep, parents commonly make some mistakes. All they want to give
their baby the best sleeping treatment but remember the obsession
can go wrong in many ways.
Therefore, here are a few things that parents need to avoid when they
are trying to make their baby sleep well.
Following a same pattern
Using the same pattern to make your baby sleep is another thing to
avoid. You can be worried if you do not know how I can make my

baby sleep. However, it is not a difficult thing at all.

In case you were able to make your baby sleep once using a pattern, then it is not confirmed that you will be able to do so all the time.

Babies require variations, their moods requirements and behaviour changes rapidly. So, you may feel frustrated in case you will not be able to succeed the same way.

Too much fancy things

Whenever you look around for the tips on how I can make my baby sleep, you will get a number of fancy tips and tricks. It is like using a lullaby, decorating a room, using different lights, bed size, bed covers, pillows and what not.

All these fancy and materialistic things can help you to some extent but these are not a complete solution. You can overburden yourself in preparing the best sleeping environment for the baby.

It will help you for a little time, not forever. You need to avoid the over-stuffing of the fancy things and tips. In fact, be real and original in creating ways for your baby to sleep well and quickly.

Playing with cognition

Commonly the tricks and tips parents use to make the baby sleep are relevant to the baby's cognition. We want to develop a consciousness

among the kids about the time to sleep.
Every parent wants their baby to sleep as soon as they tuck him or
her in the bed. It is not appropriate at all.
You should train your baby to sleep on time and wake up accordingly
but you need to make the baby understand and provide a reason for
that. Just developing a conscience is not enough; you need to create
the need for sleep in the baby as well.
Not focusing the real problem
Many people ask the question, how can I make my baby sleep.
However, most of them ignore the real problem with baby sleep. It is
not necessary that all the habits and environment is playing its part
with poor sleep.
Sometimes the problems are a little different and complicated as well.
In this manner, it is necessary to find out the real problem.
Only the investigation and consultation with experts can help you to
get the appropriate solution. Just trying out different tips and tricks will
not help you but could have worse outcomes.
Baby Sleep - Guidelines
It is always tough being a parent, though it does give you a feeling of
wholesome and satisfaction of having a family. But being a parent is
tough.

Not knowing what to do when you have recently become a parent,
many people turn to the internet or online blogs and articles for
guidelines if they don't have anyone else to ask from.
And the internet, the wondrous thing that it is, always helps some sort
of guideline to help you pass through the crises you are facing.
Many hot keywords searched on the internet about babies are often
asking how to put them to sleep. Or how to get a crying baby to sleep
in general.
This article will guide you through multiple steps on how to put your
crying baby to sleep, and hopefully, by the end of the article,
everything will be fine, and you can take a breath of relaxation.
Reasons For Crying
Babies don't cry for no reason. Since they cannot talk, they often cry
to relay their message. First and foremost is always finding out why
they are crying. It is completely necessary to remain calm as you
search for the reason. The following can be the reasons why a baby
doesn't stop crying:

- ? Fatigue.
- Sleepiness.

- ? Dirty or overfilled diaper.
- Hunger.
- ? Gas.
- ? Fear.

You have to look at the signs of what the trigger is for the baby's cries.

There is one thing to always keep in mind when the baby is crying.

NEVER SHAKE THE BABY.

Shaking your baby when you are frustrated or angry as to why the
baby hasn't stopped crying yet, will cause you and the baby problems
which will have a tragic effect. Shaking a baby may lead to brain nerve
damage, or even in some cases, these nerves explode, rendering a
baby mentally damaged, have seizures, can cause blindness, and
even death. So, never shake your baby, even in fondness. This is
called a shaken baby syndrome.

It is a given that no baby is similar to the other baby. Every child is
different, and so there might be a different method. But generally
speaking, there are several things you need to keep in mind when
your baby is continuously crying. Instead of asking oneself, how to get
a crying baby to sleep, you should try these points.

1. Stay calm

First and foremost, you always need to be calm and patient whenever
handling a baby. As they require your utmost patience and endurance
and also attention.

2. Reaching out

When you feel like everything is slipping out of your fingers. Don't
forget; you have your family and friends nearby. And if you can't reach
out to them, you can always reach out for helplines and baby
counselling available nearby you. You can always ask how to get a
crying baby to sleep. They will help you out.

3. Things to do

There are a certain number of things you can do to make your baby
stop crying.

(a)—? Swinging: if your baby doesn't stop crying, you can take them for
a ride in a car or stroller just outside the house. This creates a
swinging rhythm that lulls the baby to sleep.

(b)—? Pacifier: you can let your baby suck on a pacifier or something
resembling it, this more often than not calms the baby down.

Hopefully, this article helped you find out the solution for how to get a
crying baby to sleep. Just be patient, and you got this.

15 Tips to Better Baby Sleep - Summarised

One of the most rewarding things as a new parent is to hear

the sweet sounds of silence; that is, your baby peacefully sleeping! Every baby is unique in their sleeping habits, and it can be a tough rough for parents to navigate.

To help you achieve better baby sleep, consider these 15 tips to improve your baby's snooze sessions.

1. Consistency is Key

A bedtime routine can help a child to wind down before bed, and can also help them prepare mentally and physically for the end of the day.

Pre-bedtime activities might include a bottle, a bedtime story, and pyjamas.

When these things appear, children will know what is expected of them, and that playtime is over. Try to keep the room a little quieter when this routine begins.

2. Make Sleep Time Enjoyable

Sleep should never be seen as a bad thing in the eyes of a child.

Make bedtime a soothing, relaxing experience for them by incorporating a soothing nightlight, some natural music sounds, and their favourite blanket or stuffed animal. Nighttime should be a comforting experience for them.

As an extension of that, bedtime shouldn't always be a punishment for

children. This makes sleeping, by association, a thing that children will
want to avoid. If they're in trouble, a time-out might be more helpful.

3. Swaddle Your Baby

Especially in their first few years, children will still prefer a warm,
protective space similar to what the womb provided. Sleepsuits and
swaddles are great for keeping the baby warm and wrapped in a
comfortable position.

Swaddles can also stop babies from waking themselves up with
sudden movements and jolts, and it can even halt jumpy babies from
hitting or scratching themselves.

4. Give Children Time to Fall Asleep

The key to good sleep is to put your baby down while they're still
awake. This way, they associate their bed with the thing that makes
them cosy and sleepy.

While it is gratifying to have your child fall asleep in your arms, this
can teach them lousy sleeping habits as they get older. Having them
fall asleep in their crib will help them to become more independent
sleepers, and it will be much easier for you.

5. Give Kids a Moment

It's hard to hear a baby's cries and not tend to them-but this is precisely what you should do! If you hear your baby crying in their crib, stop and wait for a few minutes. You do not necessarily need to help them; they may already be in the habit of crying just because they don't want to go to bed yet.

Instead, wait a little while. If children need a change or have lost their soother, you can go in. However, he or she may be able to put themselves back to sleep after a few minutes, which is a huge win.

6. Don't Make Eye Contact

If your child makes eye contact with you during sleep time, they might think that it's time to wake up. If you need to go into the room for any reason, try to soothe them without looking at them, and put them back down without too much interaction.

Sooth them, but do not talk to them. Keep the room dark, so it's clear this isn't the time to be awake.

7. Refuse the Fun

Kids can easily switch off their tired mode and head back into playtime. As a parent, it's essential to try to stay calm and collected when bedtime rolls around.

Kids will try to entice you to have a giggle fest but now isn't the time.

Even if you feel guilty for not playing with them, this will

make both of
your mornings so much more manageable!

8. Avoid or Prepare for Diaper Changes

Even if you know there is going to be a mess in the morning, it is
helpful to skip diaper changes. These movements might trick your
baby into thinking it's time to wake up and play.
If it's unavoidable, have all of the necessary changing items you need
in a location outside of the bedroom. This practice will help you to
avoid spending too much time in the room looking for the items, and
you won't have to turn on the light to find anything.

9. Create a Soothing Environment

Soothing music can help to drown out other sounds around the house
and helps to put babies to sleep faster. Choose a music player that
has a few different sound options, so that you can find out what your
child likes the most.
It might be white noise, water sounds, or even a lullaby. Once they've
found something they like, have that noise playing in their bedroom
before they lie down.

10. Block Out the Light

A dark room is the best way to tell your baby that it's time to go to
sleep. Additionally, if they do happen to wake up in the middle of the

night, they'll know by the darkness that it's not time to get up yet.

Find some light-cancelling curtains that will block out the light. As they

get older, you may slowly open these curtains so that they don't get

too accustomed to complete darkness.

This will help them to stay asleep when they're in new environments

that don't have the same light-cancelling curtains.

11. Recognize a Tired Baby

If you see any sign of your baby feeling tired, whether it's a yawn or

rosy cheeks, take action right away. Timing is critical when it comes to

a baby's sleep, and if you miss your window, there's a good chance

you're in for a fussy night.

These little signs show that the body is ready for sleep, and taking

action right away will improve the chances that they easily drift off to

sleep. Waiting too long will make your baby over-tired, and wakefulness hormones will start to kick in.

At this point, it may be too late for your baby to go to sleep without

fighting. You'll get to know the signs of your baby quickly; just be sure

both parents know the signs.

12. Lower the Temperature

People of all ages tend to get better rest when they sleep in colder

temperatures. The thermostat should be between 68 and 72

Fahrenheit so that your child can experience their most comfortable rest.

Not sure if they're too cold? Lots of parents tend to feel their baby's fingers or toes when they're checking their temperature. In most cases, these body parts will feel chilly, but it doesn't mean your baby is cold.

Instead, check the temperature of your baby's chest. This part of the body is the area that will tell you if they're comfortable or not.

13. Have Necessities Ready

A full diaper might mean a massive mess in your baby's crib, but turning on the lights and trying to do a total sheet change is game over for a good sleep. Instead, be prepared with necessities always at-the-ready. To do this, you might consider putting extra sheets and swaddles in a cabinet outside of the bedroom.

You might also consider adding a waterproof pad between two sheets.

If a mess does occur, you can peel off the sheet and pad and still have a dry layer waiting underneath. Preparation will make the sheet change a quick, simple process, and your baby will be back in bed in no time.

14. Tag Team

Partners who can get a solid 5 hours of sleep each night are critical to their overall health and their performance as parents. To do this, partners must work as a team each night, even though the nursing job is a one-person show.

Partners can wait their turn, changing or soothing the baby, or whatever else is needed. Depending on work schedules, you might have varied "night shifts" so that everyone still feels rested in the morning.

15. Lead Children to the Pacifier

Lots of babies wake up in the night simply because they cannot find their pacifiers. You can fix this issue by teaching your child to learn where they can find a pacifier on their own!

Simply put pacifiers in each corner of the crib, then spend each night guiding your baby's arm to reach for the pacifiers in any corner. This practice will ensure that no matter how they twist and turn, they'll be able to locate an edge of the crib.

After about a week, they should know to reach for the corners and find the pacifier themselves. This will alleviate the need for parents to go into the bedroom at all.

A Better Sleep for All

By following these tips, not only will the baby get a night of better sleep, but her parents will, too! Consider incorporating these suggestions so that everyone gets to bed on time and wakes up feeling happy and refreshed.

Not every tip will work with your child, but it's all about patience and consistency. Work on an agreed routine and sleep schedule that works for everyone in the family.

9 798885 690799

Printed by Libri Plureos GmbH in Hamburg,
Germany